I WANT THIS
for you

Copyright © 2023 by Rumi Tsuchihashi.

All rights reserved. No part of this publication may be reproduced, distributed, or transmitted in any form or by any means, including photocopying, recording, or other electronic or mechanical methods, without the prior written permission of the publisher, except in the case of brief quotations embodied in critical reviews and specific other noncommercial uses permitted by copyright law. For permission requests, write to the publisher at the email address below.

Rumi Tsuchihashi/Tiny Wonders Press
ISBN 979-8-9897167-0-8

hello@rumitsuchihashi.com

I Want This For You: Mothering What Matters Most/

Rumi Tsuchihashi. —1st ed.

RUMI TSUCHIHASHI

I Want This For You
Mothering What Matters Most

Tiny Wonders Press

Seattle, Washington, USA

露の世は露の世ながらさりながら

-小林一作

> This world of dew
> is a world of dew,
> and yet, and yet.
>
> -Kobayashi Issa

For my mama, Noriko; my grandma, Yae; and my great-grandma, Kin. Your wisdom lives in my bones and on every page of this book.

Thank you for mothering what matters.

CONTENTS

INTRODUCTION...9

WHAT DO I MOST WANT?...13
THE FLAW IN MY INTENTION...15
BABY'S FIRST COOKING LESSON...17
THE THINGS WE DO FOR PEANUTS...21
SCRUTINY...23
NOTICE DIFFERENTLY...24
ORIGIN STORIES...26
MIRROR MIRROR...29
SPLIT SECOND CHOICE...30
BABY FEVER...32
A MINIATURE LOVE LETTER...38
BUBBLICIOUS...39
WHAT IF?...44
WARM AS FRESH DONUTS...46
EMPTY...50
(UN)WELCOME MAT...52
I'M FINE...56
POTTY PARTY...61

A STAGE AND A SEQUENCE OF EVENTS...65
INSTABILITY, DANGER, EMOTIONAL UPHEAVAL; THEN, A DECISIVE CHANGE...66
A NAVIGATION TUTORIAL...68
A NEW DAWN...72
I MISTOOK THEM FOR A NUISANCE...80
PARADISE FOUND...84
MORE THAN A BOX OF FOOD...85
ROSES AND THORNS...88
DON'T WORRY, BE HAPPY...91
SOWING THE SEEDS OF SWEETNESS...94
HOW I ANSWERED THE GOD QUESTION...98
A SHORT LIST OF SOUNDS I HOPE I'LL ALWAYS REMEMBER...99
A SOUND I WOULDN'T MIND FORGETTING...104
COME HELL OR HIGH WATER...107
I WANT THIS FOR YOU...112
PARTING WORDS + A RECIPE...118

ACKNOWLEDGMENTS...123

INTRODUCTION

I Want This For You is a book about finding yourself as you raise another human being.

Even adults who don't have offspring want "the best for the kids." But peel back the surface, and you discover what's worth wanting isn't so clear.

The everyday choices about raising kids are shockingly loaded. Is it bad to introduce a preschooler to their first taste of candy? Is a family vacation to create precious memories worth putting on a credit card? If I protest mandatory volunteering requirements, will I cause eye rolls, and will my kids stop getting invited to playdates?

The days of wrestling with such questions are long. But days turn into short years, passing by like clouds in the sky, my confidence ever shaken.

Still, I've hung in by the skin of my teeth and searched for signs of what's worth wanting. I've shed tears, raised my fists, laughed till it hurt, pressed both hands to my heart in delight at surprising moments, and taken notice.

These are my stories.

Each note, letter, and essay-ette that follows was a glimmer, a clue, or a teaching moment. The reflection spans two decades and is culled from the last five years of journaling and blogging.

I first asked, "What really matters?" in my first book, *I Want To Remember*

This. And the same question is at the heart of this book, too.

If you aren't a parent (but grew up with one), I hope you'll be inspired to unpack your childhood experiences. Consider embracing the small moments and pushing back against any standard of a good life that diminishes your joy or robs you of meaning.

And if you are a fellow parent, I wish you the same, and I offer you a permission slip to question what matters in earnest—and trust the answers that come to guide how you experience life with your children.

Now, let me take you back to 2004, when the "what matters" question began to bubble up from beneath the surface.

ONE

What do I most want?

The first Friday after I found out I was pregnant with my first child, I sat alone at the bar of a noisy, cavernous, corporate Mexican restaurant in downtown Seattle.

I waited forty-five minutes for my then-husband to arrive.

The news hadn't registered until this bit of alone time arrived. With each passing minute, the new reality was beginning to sink in.

What do I most want for this child? I asked myself. Two things immediately came to mind:

1. I want this child to grow up to be exactly, unequivocally, and unabashedly who they are.

2. I want this child to eat all foods joyfully, curiously, and adventurously.

I took a sip of iced tea and inhaled the oily, salty goodness of the tortilla chips before picking one up and scooping up a generous mound of pico de gallo. Mmm, so good.

No other thoughts followed.

So I said, "I love you already," to the peanut in my belly. "Also, consider this a warning. You'd better learn to love whatever I cook."

TWO

The flaw in my intention.

Maybe a year after this day, when I'd finally had four and a half consecutive hours of sleep for the first time in ages, I realized the flaw in my intention: I had no idea how to be myself and flourish.

How am I supposed to give a child the freedom to "be themselves" when it's something I've never experienced or understood?

By then, I'd already been introduced to the competitive notion of developmental milestones, abilities an infant is supposed to exhibit on a specific timeline. If the babies don't meet milestones, they are behind, "less than," a cause for concern.

I was obsessed with me and my kid measuring up and fitting in. My "be who you are" ideals were abstract; the mandates were not.

My infant had just had his first taste of solid mush, but I still felt hope about item number two, the loving all food part. This, at least, I could model.

I could chew, taste, savor, swallow, or spit out any food I tried. I could show the difference between yuck and yum.

One measly bit of conviction didn't feel like enough.

But it would have to do.

THREE

Baby's first cooking lesson.

The first mother-son cooking project happened when Kai was just three months old.

Cooking with an infant is a circus act. Put the baby in the vibrating hammock. Not working? Try the jumpy chair or the infant car seat and rock them with your foot as you chop, measure, wash, or stir.

I made cornbread from a box with Kai strapped into a front carrier that day. I stood at the counter at a 45-degree angle so I wouldn't squish him. I dumped the mix into the bowl, stood precariously on a stool to grab the canola oil pushed to the back of the cupboard, and cracked an egg (my single-handed cracking skills are weak, but I managed).

When it came time to stir things together, I needed one hand to hold the bowl. I couldn't do that at this awkward angle. So, I stood straight, moved the bowl to where I could feel it on my left, and reached around the baby with my right arm to whisk the batter.

I couldn't see what I was doing—Kai's head blocked my view. But I could tell something was off. The mixture was too thick. Then I remembered I forgot to add water!

So, I let the whisk rest inside the bowl while I fixed that problem. But when I reached around Kai again, the whisk wasn't where I left it. I searched with my left hand. Still no whisk. Then, I felt the bowl move.

The baby had grabbed it—and he was now stirring things up with a lot of vigor for a small baby. All excited, I called his father over to capture this moment. Baby's first cooking lesson was happening on the fly!

I still have that picture somewhere.

If I dig it out, I'll see dark circles under my eyes, greasy hair, and a hard-won and effervescent smile of a woman who hasn't yet registered what else is in the frame of that shot: next to the stainless-steel bowl is a hideous pile, stuff that doesn't even belong in the kitchen—like laundry detergent and screwdrivers, not the cocktail kind—captured for eternity.

The sight of such things would be so ghastly that the cute pic would never even make it onto the fridge.

Not then, not ever.

This is too bad because if I could look beyond the imperfections, I'd see Kai's chubby little hands gripping the whisk with all his might, showing his eagerness to feel his way around the kitchen and the world beyond.

FOUR

The things we do for peanuts.

People didn't visit the dentist much in post-depression-era Tokyo. *Obaachan*, my maternal grandmother, appears to have all her teeth in my baby pictures—she was in her fifties then, just a bit older than I am now—but by the time we moved in with her when I was nine, quite a few of them were missing.

She tried valiantly to wear her dentures so she could properly chew. Sometimes, she'd spend half an hour in front of the mirror trying to fit them in her tiny mouth. She always gagged. When she could finally tolerate the torturous thing, she'd gently put five or six roasted peanuts, *ojiichan's* favorite snack, into her palm and pop them into her mouth.

The semi-grounded contents would tumble into a thin hand towel seconds later.

Whenever I think of the bathroom sink in my grandmother's house, I think of the painfully pink and ill-fitting plastic torture device in a shallow glass water dish at my eye level. It rarely left that spot.

I wonder what object sits quietly in this house where I write, speaking volumes about me, that my son and daughter take for granted now but will recall many years later.

FIVE

Scrutiny.

We were in the restroom of a chain store—famous for its trademarked use of the color red—the first time I changed Kai's diaper in public.

As I laid his 20-inch-long body down on a crunchy nylon mat, a random older lady stood by close enough to breathe down my neck. She scolded me for being out with a baby so young and critiquing my every move.

So, this is how it is. My parental intentions—they are good, aren't they?—are subject to public scrutiny. Anytime, anywhere.

SIX

Notice differently.

Dear Kai and Reina,

Today, if you provide commentary on anything, can you notice what's right? Even if this something technically doesn't meet your standard of excellence?

Say you were served foul food on a long international flight. "The tray sure is sturdy" or "The roll has a pleasant shape" is a terrific start. Try it, even if it feels forced or silly.

This is surprisingly hard to do, to be that specific with what's right.

But I beg you to try.

It's a kind thing to do for others. It's also a challenging thing to do for ourselves, as you'll see when you get older and accumulate a history of mistakes and imperfections. This isn't your fault, really—schools and workplaces all contribute to this imbalance in what we notice.

Young as you are, you may already have an easier time finding fault than compliments. But you are so much more than the history of mistakes and imperfections you carry around.

You are good.

Look for what's good.

Mama

SEVEN

Origin stories.

The summer before he started kindergarten, Kai asked me, "How did the universe begin?"

It was well past his bedtime—again. And this seemed like one of those times when giving a bullshit answer would bite me in the ass later, and he'd find out I didn't know what I was talking about.

"Well, it began in an explosion," I said. "Scientists call it the Big Bang. Would you like me to read you books about the Big Bang?"

He let me leave his bedside without a fuss after this question. I felt giddy. I took him to the library the next day.

Eager to show off this deep-thinking five-year-old, I made Kai restate his question to the librarian. I wish I had a picture of the man behind the desk, pulling his reading glasses down to help him see this sweetly serious-looking child with sparkly eyes.

Kai and I checked out one book that day, and over the next four weeks, I got more and more notices about picture books on hold in our names.

By early August, we'd read well over two dozen such books. When I asked, Kai said yes; he felt his question had been fully answered.

That night, I got to feel like the most brilliant, best mom on the planet. Look at me; I'm nailing this mothering with intent business!

Two days later, Kai tugged at my shirt when I passed him in the hallway.

"Mama," he asked, "How do you know God is real? It's not like you can see or touch God."

The origin story requests never end.

EIGHT

Mirror mirror.

The first time newborn Reina met her brother, at barely 30 minutes old, she mimicked her brother's facial expressions with incredible precision.

This was before I learned about mirror neurons, the reflexive act of copying what we see, a hardwiring of the brain.

I didn't need to know the science to appreciate what was unfolding before my eyes—the baked-in impulse to learn human-ing by behaving like those around you.

Reina's actions looked so effortless it gave me the chills.

NINE

Split second choice.

The almost-three-year-old looked me in the eye, then barreled down hilly Crocket Street. He was headed for the busy intersection at Queen Anne Avenue.

I was standing idly on the sidewalk holding a pink gingham infant car seat with a sleeping nine-week-old inside. Together, my "baggage" weighed thirty pounds. I couldn't run fast enough with the baby in tow.

Do I endanger the infant by leaving her unattended, or risk running too slow, too far behind the toddler, and letting him get hit by a car?

My mind froze, unable to make
a choice.

So, my body did the choosing for me.
My legs took off sprinting. Both arms
outstretched to catch the little shit.

I watched the toes of his light-up
sneaker come within inches of the
street. My fingers didn't quite reach.
My vision blurred.

But when all seemed lost, the little
tyrant threw me for a loop again.

He pivoted, made a ninety-degree left
turn, and continued his terror run
down the other sidewalk.

TEN

Baby fever.

My daughter wanted nothing more than to have a baby doll, and then another baby doll, and then another baby doll.

Not just to collect them but to have them with her and always tend to.

When Reina was four and five, going out for a walk looked like this: we'd unfold the toy double stroller into which four babies would go—one in the seat, one in the backseat, and two in the basket underneath the undercarriage. Then, Reina would strap a baby onto her backpack, the special American Girl brand kind with a

built-in carrier affixed to the front.
Once securely fastened, one more baby
would be slipped into the zipper
compartment with its head
sticking out.

Finally, she would carefully wrap
another baby doll in a thin blanket and
tuck it inside her sweatshirt.

So, at minimum, every walk involved
preparing seven baby dolls, sometimes
eight, to join our adventure before we
could get out the door. I marveled at
this ritual and its over-the-top
cuteness. I also felt a mild disgust.

Why disgust? For one, getting out the
door took a lot of work.

Second, raising a daughter so into
caretaking as an imaginary play made

me seem un-feminist. Of course, I wanted her to care for young, vulnerable things, but the extent of Reina's obsession made me queasy.

I wasn't a doll-loving child myself. I didn't get doll play. And why so darned many babies every single time?

It would take well over a decade before I had my answer.

No, I wasn't a woman who nurtured imaginary babies as a child. But I was a woman who was always carrying many babies with her.

I carried the responsibility for Reina, her older brother, her older half-sister, and several inner children: the baby that lives inside of me, her father's inner baby, and countless other inner children of family members who were yearning to be tended to.

These babies were always with me. I never left home without them, not even one.

Everywhere I went, I carried a load of babies with me.

During all those walks, if Reina was obsessing about anything, it was about reflecting the world—and me—exactly as she saw it.

Show them how to cry
when pets and people die.
*Show them the infinite pleasure
in the touch of a hand.*
And make the ordinary
come alive for them.

———

WILLIAM MARTIN

ELEVEN

A miniature love letter.

May this note remind you to cherish the little moments. Your most ordinary experiences are wondrous one-time miracles, a portal for love and connection. Savor them. Share them. Let them hold your attention.

TWELVE

Bubblicious.

Dear Reina,

The girl from the opposing team broke away from the crowd and kicked the ball far forward. Between her and the goal was an open soccer field—and you.

You were a head taller than the girl coming your way and taller than most of the girls on either team. You looked imposing. Everyone thought you would stop the other girl's momentum and keep the opposing team from scoring.

We watched you run for the ball. We watched the other girl run for the ball. It looked like some bodily contact and a hustle would be imminent.

The mothers on your team shouted, "Go Reina, go Reina!"

But instead of a tough fight, we witnessed you step aside and clear an open path to the goal. Scooooore! For the other team!

The same mothers who just seconds ago were shouting your name moaned. I felt the weight of their frustration and disappointment like a heavy cloak.

After we lost the game, I pulled you aside when you and your teammates were happily eating grapes and goldfish crackers and drinking apple juice from a box.

"Hey, Reina," I asked. "What happened when that other girl came towards you to score a goal?"

"Oh," you said, your eyes bright with pride. "I stayed in my bubble, Mama. Just like my kindergarten teacher says. I stayed in my bubble!"

Stayed in my bubble? Are you kidding me?

"But soccer is different," I snapped.

"Different?" you asked, eyebrows furrowed, your light and confidence dimming before my eyes.

"Different?" you said once more.

I changed the subject and let you go back to your friends. As if to say, forget it, it's no big deal, but I remember that day so clearly.

Standing on the sidelines, I thought, "You should know that a soccer game has temporary rules that aren't like the rest of your life." I thought that you should care to know the difference between life and game rules, and from now on, forget "staying in your bubble" during soccer, forget courtesy and personal space for a second, and do what's more likely to bring victory to the team.

The thing is, I need help understanding the boundaries between the field and life, even now. When grown-ups tell children to "just play the game" about life, not sports, I feel confused, even disgusted.

I would prefer if we all stayed in our bubble without exception.

But I had this idea that I had to protect you from a harshly judging world by making you behave like you cared about winning more than bubbles.

As if, at five years old, you didn't already know better.

Ever learning,

Mama

THIRTEEN

What if?

If I hadn't
been born in the seventies,
grew up moving between Japan and
the States,
watched my mother stare
absentmindedly at the horizon while I
gingerly tugged on her tailored
homemade skirts,
then stuck my nose in a book to hide
my sorrows.

If I hadn't
been the oldest of three kids,
who was terrible at any sport
involving balls,
but got a high from doing for others
what they can do for themselves.

If work culture hadn't pressured my
father to be one of the too many
blacked-out drunks,
nor pressured women with children to
be affluent do-it-alls or picture-perfect
stay-at-homes,

if then
would I recognize what matters,
and what's worth wanting,
with precision and ease?

FOURTEEN

Warm as fresh donuts.

It was an ordinary morning in January, gray and bitterly cold. I piled the kids into the car and went to the neighborhood donut shop.

That sounds idyllic, doesn't it? I assure you it was not.

"Did you get your socks?" I asked a dozen times before our departure.

"What do you mean you got them out of the drawer, but now you don't know where they went?" I yelled, eventually clipping the child into the booster seat, barefoot inside the dinosaur rainboots, with unmatched socks I'd retrieved from the laundry basket tossed onto his lap.

We finally get to the donut shop, where the kind person behind the counter seems to notice my furrowed brow and smiles weakly, a look of pity.

The kids pick a cozy spot beside a wall-to-wall shelf full of antique books. They drop big crumbs all over the table as we eat, sip our warm drinks, giggle, and talk. After it happened once accidentally, the kids roll a pen off the table on purpose to see how far it'll go; a stupid game I'm too defeated to stop.

I stand up to put my coat on.

"Excuse me," a woman seated near me pipes up. My body instantly stiffens, anticipating criticism. So many strangers seem entitled to share a piece of their mind with mothers they don't know.

"I don't mean to alarm you," she says (which totally alarms me), "but I've been noticing how you interact with your children."

Here we go. I hold my breath.

"You're so respectful of them. And kind. You show your kids that what they have to say matters."

This is unexpected. I cock my head in confusion.

"Thank you for showing up," she continues, reaching out to take my hand into hers for a gentle squeeze. "You really made my day."

I really made her day.

This defeated version of me, holding on for dear life, made her day.

I can't register her words, but I feel her touch, her palm in mine, soft and warm as the fresh donuts had been. And equally warm tears well up, threatening to spill over.

FIFTEEN

Empty.

Me (half asleep with the lights still on, drool on the pillow, and one eye cracked open): "What's going on?"

Kai: "I can't sleep."

Me: "I can see that. What's making it so hard to sleep?"

Kai: "I feel empty."

Me (sitting up now): "You feel what? Empty? Empty how?"

Kai (one hand on his chest, staring out the window, taking a deep breath in):

"I feel empty
like a piggy bank
with no money inside.

I feel empty
like a sandwich
with no filling

I feel empty
that's how I feel."

SIXTEEN

(Un) welcome mat.

We were at *that* chain store (which made the color red famous) again.

To the right of the entrance stood the $1 section and their bins and bins of tempting knickknacks. It's so easy to casually toss a thing or two into your empty shopping cart. Don't resist, grease the consumer wheels!

And so it was that shopping with Kai at this store involved picking up a toy—something that he'd be bored of before he even got home and added to the clutter at home—because, hey, why make a big deal over one measly dollar?

But I'd had enough.

This time, I was determined. We would not be shopping from the dollar section.

But of course, there had to be wooden choo choo trains right at the two-year-old's eye level that day. Of course, Kai insisted he absolutely had to have that train.

"Not today, Kai," I said with all the firmness I could muster. "Let's go over to the cracker section. I'll let you pick out your favorite kind of goldfish."

"No!" he screamed. "I want train! I want *this* train!"

I didn't waiver, but neither did Kai.

After the twenty-fifth round, Kai got momentarily quiet. He waddled over to the welcome mat. He proceeded to flop around like a shrimp out of water and shrieked. Loudly. While the automatic doors opened and closed.

One unsuspecting shopper after another walked in the glass doors, most of them in a daze. They were startled by the sight of a convulsing toddler, his booming voice, and the crocodile tears streaming down his face.

Some jumped over Kai, others tip-toed around. Every person looked at me with the vertically turned eyes of an angry goat; a few admonished me out loud. I said little in return.

It's incredible how even an agonizing scene like this can put you in a trance.

Twenty minutes later, this toddler, who seemed committed to throwing a tantrum for life, right there at the entrance, with the automatic doors opening and closing, opening and closing forever, suddenly shot up, got within inches of me,
and whispered,

"Mama, let's goldfish."

It was my turn to be scared awake.

SEVENTEEN

I'm fine.

Once, my family summered at a cabin on Lopez Island with a private beach. My then-in-laws bought this vacation at a charity auction and invited their children to share it. Twelve of us joined under a single roof.

I was freshly postpartum. At the trip's start, my second child was fourteen days old. I also had a two-and-a-half-year-old son I'd cared for alone in the last months of my pregnancy.

The three things I remember most about this trip are:

1. How the two boats we brought along both broke down.

2. What little I saw of the men, the father of my children included.

3. Making a giant batch of chicken salad.

Back then, I breastfed every few hours. I was sleeping maybe three hours a night, four if you include the five-minute catnaps (aka passing out on the couch.) My maternity clothes hung awkwardly on my lumpy frame, and my hips, back, neck, and perineum were sore.

The exhaustion was real, and the vulnerability was visceral. I felt the way a wounded pup looks.

And yet, I was in the kitchen, chopping grapes, red onions, parsley, and celery, crumbling walnuts, and emulsifying a mayo and red wine vinegar dressing.

I was pushing myself to the brink to prove that I was "fine." My protective instinct was on fire, and I was driven to ensure everyone knew I was a productive, useful member of this tribe. Someone who, whatever the circumstances, brought something to the table. Quite literally.

There's such a seduction to saying, "I'm fine" to other people, even when we're not.

There's such an ego boost in proving it with grand gestures of productivity.

I couldn't have known it at the time. Still, by making that chicken salad—sweet and savory, with a silky dressing, toothy with a nice crunch, herby with a hint of black pepper heat, a self-esteem-boosting creation to be sure—I leveled up my bullshit tolerance. I created a body memory of performative showing up that denied what was true: I needed rest. I needed to be safe in my physical distress.

For years to come, I called on this body memory of faux-unbotheredness to slog through rough patches. I invested in proving my toughness for toughness's sake and called it good mothering.

Balderdash, I say.

So, as delicious as it was, if I could turn back time, I wouldn't make the salad.

It wasn't worth it.

EIGHTEEN

Potty party.

The summer Kai was three-and-a-half, I was rather desperate. By then, he'd been almost potty trained for most of a year. Which is to say, I was throwing away whole outfits—from shirts to socks—almost weekly, thanks to his beyond-cleanable accidents.

(If you've been around a boy this age, you know what I'm talking about. If you haven't, well, know I'm not exaggerating. At all.)

One day, an image flashed in my mind—a kind of game board with ten squares plus another big one at the end. The big square was half-covered

with a picture of an ecstatic Curious George holding a bouquet of balloons and featuring the words
POTTY PARTY!!!

And so I got to work making that vision a reality. By that evening, the game board image was stuck to our fridge with plastic alphabet magnets.

"You see this, Kai?" I pointed to the eleventh square, "You make it to the bathroom ten times, and you're gonna get a party to celebrate!"

Kai looked at me, looked at the board, put his finger on George's face, and then glanced back at me sternly. "You said party," he grumbled. "Will there be cake?"

Eight of us gathered at my neighbor's house less than a month later. Their kitchen table was festive: covered with kazoos, shiny paper plates, the now-sticker-covered game board from the fridge, and yes, a cake—with the proud inscription in blue cursive, "Happy Potty, Kai!!!"

I explained the occasion to the kids old enough to understand. Then we lit a candle and sang the birthday song with the lyrics swapped.

Sometimes, people ask me if I thought Kai deserved a party for his achievement. I look at them like they're nuts. But then again, I've never asked friends to help me celebrate cleaning up my own messes, even metaphorically speaking.

Why the stinginess? Why can't we whoop it up because we wiped our butts without making a big deal ten times in a row?

Growing up is all about wiping poop off our asses again and again and again. Cleaning, cleansing, and facing the unpleasant parts of life are the hallmarks of a responsible grown-up. What's wrong with celebrating this essential life skill?

I have no answers, but I say it's time to push against the norm.

Let's have ourselves a Potty Party today.

NINETEEN

A stage and a sequence of events.

One day, I asked the voice behind my Echo device this question.

Me: "Alexa, what's the definition of a crisis?"

Alexa: "A crisis can be defined as a stage and a sequence of events that determine the trend of future occurrences, particularly for better or worse. It signifies a period of instability, danger, or emotional upheaval that can lead to a decisive change."

Whoa. With blinking eyes, I asked her if she'd please repeat what she just said.

TWENTY

Instability, danger, emotional upheaval; then, a decisive change.

I hoped with all my heart that my children's first home would be their forever home. Having grown up moving from house to house until we took refuge in my grandparents' place, a forever home for my babes was one of my most fervent wishes.

Things did not work out that way.

When I couldn't cling to hope anymore, I whitewashed every wall in every room with gallons of mid-grade eggshell latex paint from a big box store and put the house on the market.

All evidence of our lives there got erased in about 48 hours. But there was one small exception.

When the house sold three days later, the kids' heights were still pencil-marked and dated on the kitchen doorframe.

One evidence of our timeline I couldn't bear to erase.

TWENTY-ONE

A navigation tutorial.

Dear Kai and Reina.

At first, everything was easy.

We were cruising along Lake Union slowly enough not to create a wake. And the captain—your dad, who was napping in the focsle—had set up the autopilot so the boat could practically drive itself to the dock.

The one task beyond the machine was scanning the water for kayakers or other erratically moving boats. That left me plenty of time to soak in the gorgeousness of the glittering Seattle skyline. Occasionally, I'd gaze at the autopilot screen in the dash to see how we were doing.

Near the bottom of the screen was a vaguely triangular shape. The triangle was connected to a straight line, our navigational course. Early on, I noticed the triangle tip pointed too much to the left. Even after several minutes, it didn't fix itself.

"Dumb autopilot," I said under my breath, "I have to do your work for you." Then I grabbed the steering wheel and turned it twenty or so degrees to the right. Problem solved.

As the minutes passed, the pink streaks in the sky faded to a swath of dark purple. By then, the supposedly automated navigation system had become a constant irritant. It showed no interest in aligning the point of the triangle with the course line.

And for some infuriating reason, the gauge would show a later-than-before estimated arrival time each time I straightened things up. And the fuel consumption estimate went up, too.

Eventually, your dad must have heard my complaints. He came up from the lower cabin. "Stop touching the steering wheel," he told me matter-of-factly.

"Stop touching it so much and see what happens," he repeated.

So now I know. Autopilots are off-course 99% of the time. They're designed to be responsive to their immediate environments and adjust to minimize resistance. All the while, they keep track of the destination. Even though they behave like they're going the wrong way, they aren't.

In case you're wondering if, because of the divorce, my memories of being with your dad are all bad, there's something you should know.

Oddly enough, he was the one who prepared me to make a necessary life course correction.

That evening on the boat and through the GPS, your dad had shown me how to lean into the uncertainty to come, trust guidance, and keep the fear of moving forward in check.

Mama

TWENTY-TWO

A new dawn.

At one point, I fell asleep nightly with my clothes still on, only to wake up soon after and frantically write in my journal.

"Who are you to break up the family when you don't know how it'll affect them?"

"What kind of mother becomes the source of her children's pain?"

Stuff like that.

One morning after one of those nights, I enrolled eleven-year-old Kai in a tiny private middle school, hopeful that this school situation would mitigate some of the pain of his father moving out. But best intentions notwithstanding, by mid-November, I got the fourth unsettling phone call from school in a month. I let out a blood-curdling scream the minute I hung up.

My unsuspecting child bounded in the door an hour later. "Hi, Mom!"

"Your teacher called again," I launched in, voice shaking, not even returning the hello.

"What's going on? You won't turn your work in at the end of class. They say they've done everything they've done to help you. Now they think you're just unmotivated. Is that true? That's not okay! What are you going to do, Kai?"

I say all this without taking a breath, tears stinging my eyes.

Kai, understandably, stares at me. Then, after a few seconds of stunned silence, he asks me a haunting question.

"Mom, why do you care what the teachers think so much?"

I stand there in front of my kid, chin drooping. I can't form a coherent response. The best I can do is mumble about returning to this conversation later.

I stumble to my bedroom, then draw the curtains with a dramatic whoosh before getting into bed. I pull the covers over my head. I'm aware that my feelings are bigger than the situation warrants, but I cannot stuff them back inside.

Something about Kai's question has unmoored me. "Rumi, what the hell," I say to myself.

Why do I care so much about what the teachers think?

The hours tick by. Amber light enters the window at a steep angle. I know it's time to cook, but my body, tear-soaked and sweaty, is immobile. I'm only half awake, and it's helping me contemplate that piercing question.

I wanted to impress the teachers. I admit to myself. I wanted to show them I had it together and that I was not ruining my child's life, not by a long shot. I was upset at my kid for not complying, for not doing what "well-adjusted" children do, and for ruining my cover and crumbling my facade.

"Don't wake her up," I hear Kai telling his sister. He must have peeked at me through a crack in the door.

Downstairs, the fridge opens and closes; drawers open and shut. The faucet turns on and off, first in the kitchen, then upstairs in the bathroom. I hear tip toes of kid-sized feet in the hallway. Then, silence.

Dusk turns into a long, fitful night. I rise early, sneak into Kai's room, then Reina's, and watch the sunrise over their soft faces and heaving chests.

"I want to talk about what happened yesterday," I say to Kai when he gets home the next day.

Without a word, he plops himself on the couch, looks me in the eye, and motions for me to sit beside him. It's the second beginning of a new dawn.

Whatever happens
to you belongs to you.
Make it yours.
Feed it to yourself
even if it feels impossible
to swallow. Let it nurture you
because it will.

———

CHERYL STRAYED

TWENTY-THREE

I mistook them for a nuisance.

I'm with Reina, calming her down so she can fall asleep, and Kai barges into her room. Once, twice, three times.

He interrupts us with random questions every single time. We ignore him the first two times, but on the third, he asks, "Is this real?" and points to a tiny vial full of glinting gold, a souvenir from a tourist gift shop in Long Beach, Oregon. When he brings it close to our faces, we can't help but stop the conversation admire and this tiny beauty.

Encouraged by our reaction, Kai leaves again, and soon, he's back again.

I moan. I want long, drawn-out bedtimes with Reina to be over with—she's ten years old, for crying out loud—to luxuriate in a few minutes of solo freedom. These antics aggravate me; they get under my skin.

This time, Kai is gleefully clutching a long-lost wallet. And I soon discover it's a bona fide treasure trove, even more full of gold than that vial.

We find three small pieces of paper inside the billfold, receipts from when the kids and I visited Tokyo in the fall of 2017. Each one is a miniature chronicle.

I read each line to the kids since they don't read or speak Japanese. It shows we were at the 7-Eleven a few blocks from my parent's house at 11:25 a.m. on

November 21, and Kai had spent his last bit of yen on Lemon Coke and chocolate-dipped potato chips.

Reading aloud leads to a flood of sensations and brings me back to the scene. I see the bright sunlight streaming into the store that morning and the warmth on my cheeks. I smell *oden* cooking in a large stainless-steel pot. I feel the steam rising from behind the cashier as she rings up these items. I hear the little yips and whoops Kai and Reina made, the sound of skipping feet on the road that led back to Jiji and Baba's house.

First, Kai brought us "real gold," still confined in a tiny vial.

Then, he brought us a lost wallet, unlocked a precious memory from its confines, and let all kinds of riches spill over.

And to think that I wanted togetherness at bedtime over with. To think I wanted Kai to go away and stop interrupting. To think I wanted out of the here and now so I could be "free."

TWENTY-FOUR

Paradise found.

Maybe it doesn't matter where we are—we find paradise when we aren't too quick to decide that things are wrong or terrible and instead follow the unfolding story with curiosity.

Maybe we experience paradise when we have room in our hearts and minds for everything, even people who act in a way that's hard for us to take.

Maybe paradise happens when we say yes to this moment, precisely as it is.

TWENTY-FIVE

More than a box of food.

Dear Kai,

Do you know how I still pack your and your sister's lunches? I know I could ask you to do this on your own, but there's a reason why I have a hard time letting this job go.

Obaachan, your great grandma, used to pack my school lunches. Beautiful bento boxes with a main course and veggies and fruit. She did this during my middle school years until I was about fifteen.

One day, I told her I wanted to lose weight. I said I wanted my lunches to have fewer calories. She tried to help me do that for a while, but one day, she told me, "I don't know how to do this for you. If you want things done your way, you must do it yourself."

And just like that, I was in charge of this task every morning.

At first, I felt empowered. I used this 1,200-calories-a-day cookbook to create normal-looking lunches (I didn't want any classmates to know I was on a diet) that helped control my appetite and shrink my body. I liked being able to do something difficult until I didn't.

Eventually, I gave up on being skinny. But *obaachan's* work was done—the lunches she packed were a thing of the past. Soon, she was too sick to make them for me even if she wanted to.

Part of why I pack your lunches is because I still mourn the abrupt ending of something I loved but took for granted.

Only when they were gone did I realize every lunch *obaachan* made me was a love letter.

Mama

TWENTY-SIX

Roses and thorns.

Reina and I have a nighttime ritual called "Roses and Thorns."

A rose is something from the day that was inspiring, felt good, or made us grateful. A thorn is a frustration, disappointment, or a struggle. We take turns sharing.

"My thorn today," I said one evening not too long ago, "isn't just a thorn for today. It's a thorn that's been getting bigger and pointier for a while." We were lying on my bed, heads almost touching, staring up at the shadows on the ceiling.

I could feel Reina's eyes turn towards me, even as I kept my gaze fixed upward. I felt beads of cold sweat form under my armpits.

"I was pretty proud of my first draft," I said, referring to stories I'd passed onto a coworker for feedback. "But all the comments were about what wasn't right. Not one of the comments pointed out something good."

You put periods at the end of bullet points. At this organization, we don't do that.

The quote you picked isn't compelling.

Are you sure you just uploaded the latest version of the document? The same errors from before are still there.

"The more I got attention on my mistakes, the more I started making them," I said, my voice quivering. "And now I feel like I can't do anything right."

"Oh, Mom," Reina responds softly. I hear a tiny sniffle.

Of course, she knows what I'm talking about. This is how her life goes every day, with all those graded assignments just as it did in school for most of us, too, when we were kids, leaving us fearful of making mistakes and being punished.

When I finally mustered the courage to turn my head sideways and face Reina, a single tear rolled onto her pillow.

That's when I noticed the trail of her single tear. We were mirror images.

TWENTY-SEVEN

Don't worry, be happy.

When I first woke up, nothing seems amiss.

I hear the same cacophony of children's voices and smell the same fast food. It's as if only seconds have passed.

I raise my head. I see the sky. And I notice how the true blue of high noon has given way to the lilac hues of an impending sunset.

When I cup my face in astonishment, the fingertips on my left hand graze a deep indent on my cheek. I remember laying down my backpack on top of the picnic table. I must have turned that backpack into an impromptu pillow.

And passed out cold from stress and exhaustion. I blink.

Then, a chilling thought comes over me. "The children, where are my children?"

I came here with my eleven and eight-year-old. Where are they?

I scan the sea of heads with black hair attached to tiny humans—child after child, not mine. My heart palpates.

But then, I see a low wall in the distance through my misty eyes. And on top of that wall are two familiar faces, beaming and playing what looks like a made-up game.

This scene looks different from what a parent-child outing to Tokyo Disneyland should be. The brochure version of the Happiest Place on Earth doesn't involve an unconscious parent, a four-hour stay at the food court, or children inventing play activities instead of watching parades or going on fantastic rides.

And yet, and yet.

You couldn't find two happier faces than those two over there anywhere in the whole theme park, not even in the brochure.

TWENTY-EIGHT

Sowing the seeds of sweetness.

"I just thought of something," Reina says from the passenger seat as I turn left onto busy Mercer Street.

"Remember that time we planted seeds in flowerpots at preschool?"

"Mm, hm," I say and nod.

It's been twelve years, but I still remember the activity. I remember how my neck itched, and my stomach got queasy then. I'd lied to kids that day.

After the toddlers left the classroom for the day, Linda, the preschool teacher, played a little magic trick, which the adults were in on.

"I was so shocked to see a swirly lollipop growing out of my pot when we came back to school, Mom," Reina says. She's fiddling with her seatbelt as she talks.

At the time, I had reservations about the adults magic-ing the seeds to grow fast and for the seeds to yield candy on a stick. I felt the little ones deserved to know how seeds are—they have enormous potential but might not sprout despite our best efforts. I'm surprised how strongly I feel about this decision to skirt "the truth" all these years later.

"Looking back, do you feel like we lied to you?" I ask.

The cars ahead make erratic lane changes as we near the freeway onramp. The tension on the road adds an extra strain to the long silence.

"Mm, I don't know about that," Reina says, finally. "It felt like love, like everything about those preschool times did. Just love."

The kids planted curiosity, tended to it, and then let it go. They learned that sweetness, sometimes in surprising forms, grows when they do this. Which is a lesson on hope and love as valid as "how seeds work."

The two truths were layered, revealed over time, and never in conflict. I get this now in a way that Reina may have already had long ago.

Back home, I dig the dirt up in my tiny yard and prepare the soil to receive a fresh batch of seeds. I want candy-sweet goodness to grow from my efforts, too.

TWENTY-NINE

How I answered the God question.

"Kai," I said, feigning confidence,
though I don't know what to say next.

"How do you know God is real? You
know, the same way you know love is
real. You can't see or touch love either,
right? But you can feel it in your heart."

Kai closes his eyes, puts his right hand
on his chest, and swooshes with his
mouth like he's tasting something
sweet. Sweet, like his favorite
gummy candy.

"Mmm," he moans.

And I think, Hallelujah.

THIRTY

A short list of sounds I hope I'll always remember.

Fall leaves crunching under firefighter rainboots on a perfectly sunny day.

The voicemail greeting I recorded with Kai ("Pweaze weave us a message!")

Kai's man-sized hand patting the open seat on the couch as he cues up another episode of *Family Guy* on the TV.

The whoosh of a collective exhales from the backseat as we exit the long, long tunnel, and Reina and her bestie stop holding their breaths.

The toilet flushing, and the sink water turning on seconds later.

The ding of that first text message, five days after the kids left for a trip to Tanzania without me.

Water splashes three feet high as Reina jumps off the edge of the high diving board and lands butt-first in the pool—the third time a charm.

Tiny snores came from 22-inch bodies in the early afternoon.

The hush on Christmas Eve after Reina finally falls asleep in her makeshift bed in the hallway (ten steps closer to the tree than sleeping in her room.)

The humming sound, *nyom nyom nyom nyom*, Kai makes even now when the food is delicious.

Reina (4): "Kai, what's Bieber fever?"

Kai (6): Gulps his apple juice. "It's when you listen to Justin Bieber's music too much and it makes you sick."

Bitty stocking feet against the hardwood floor, pushing to reach new heights in the bouncy chair.

The pencil sliding against that same door frame to mark their heights.

Usher's *DJ Got Us Fallin' In Love* booming in the kitchen, because it's a spontaneous dance party and we've got the bass turned way up.

The piece of paper rustling in the wind as Reina walks back to the car, proving she passed the driver's test.

The slap of his small palm on mine when Kai manages to tie his shoelaces all by himself.

Kai begging for a *debedebede* (DVD) at the library.

Mr. Rose, the second-grade teacher, cracking up loudly in the elementary school hallway as he imitates Kai's spot-on imitation of Steve Martin as The Pink Panther.

The bicycle tires rolling steadily against the asphalt for the first time.

"Bye," and the kitchen door clicking shut. This means Reina willingly walked herself to middle school instead of begging me to drive to spare her a ten-minute walk.

Sniffles now spaced five seconds apart after a hard, half-hour-long cry.

"I did it!"

"Thank you."

"I wub you."

THIRTY-ONE

A sound I wouldn't mind forgetting.

Momomomomomomomomomomo
momomomomomomomomomomo
momomomomomomomomomomo
momomomomomomomomomomo
momomomomomomomomomomo
momomomomomomomomomomo
momomomomomomomomomom!

Oft hope is born *when all is* forlorn.

J.R.R. TOLKIEN

THIRTY-TWO

Come hell or high water.

It's early December 2020, nine months into Covid-19 lockdown.

Nothing about our impending holiday season is the same. There are no places to go and no people to see—not that I did too much going out or seeing people on a "normal" year, what between the divorce and the complicated co-parenting logistics this time of year and the kids turning into teens who won't do things just because their parents want to anymore.

But I did have an ongoing tradition of taking pictures with Santa. I'd kept it up for sixteen consecutive years. And petty as it sounds, given the gravity of Covid worldwide, I was deflated about this streak ending. I was not okay with this precious thread of joy being broken.

I told Kai about the end of Santa photos one morning. He'd just turned sixteen; not only did I not expect him to care, I thought I'd get a barely concealed eye roll. But upon hearing the news, Kai puffed his chest, leaned close, and said he was not ready to give up.

Just hours later, I received very good news. A local photographer says he's rented a well-ventilated studio space and figured out a safe, socially distanced way to do Santa portraits for one week only! My heartbeat quickens.

The only appointment left is midday Thursday. I'm on thin ice with my boss, but I'm willing to fake a last-minute doctor's visit to make this happen. And I'll let the kids skip online school while I'm at it.

This is a much-needed win in an exhausting year of uncertainty and loss. Woot! I hollered when the confirmation popped up on my phone screen.

The day comes.

A deluge has hit. It is wet, even for Seattle, world-famous for the copious amount of rain it gets. I peek out the window and see ankle-deep sheets of water streaming down the slopey street. The force is so intense that the drain in front of the house is bubbling.

I hear Reina belatedly fixing her hair. I tense up at the sound; we need to head out in five minutes. Then Kai yells, "Mom, Mom, come look at this!"

And what do I see but an exploding toilet! There is a ferocious, shit-brown geyser shooting three feet high in the air.

Oh. Crap.

My mind quiets for three seconds, with Kai standing behind me and peering over my shoulders.

One thing is for sure: I can't call an emergency plumber and make this photo appointment. I only have time to do one or the other.

"What are we gonna do, Mom?" Kai asks as the foul-smelling liquid spills onto the linoleum floor and creepily oozes toward us.

I blink, then grab the doorknob.

I hear a satisfying click.

Then, I lean my forehead against the door for support.

"Kai," I say, turning toward him, "we're going to take pictures with Santa."

In the face of an uncontrollable shitstorm, I decide to run toward joy once and for all.

THIRTY-THREE

I want this for you.

So here we are, driving to a friend's house, an elementary school reunion slash early high school graduation party. Kai is in the passenger seat for the first time in forever.

The most logical route takes us to our old house. The house I brought him back to the day after he was born, the one I fought to keep after the divorce but couldn't and sold to another family.

And for three years, we lived next door to this old house. (Yes, it was awkward, but our friends offered the rental at a rate I could afford, and that move kept the disruption in my kids' lives at a bare minimum, all things considered.)

"There it is," Kai says, pointing happily to the siding, painted a shade of gray I'd painstakingly picked out from a dozen swatches.

I can't look.

"Hey, Mom," Kai asks after we're half a block away. "Did I ever tell you about the time I walked into our old house?"

He hasn't. But for a month or two after the move, we were still cleaning up the dust and debris, and I often forgot to lock the door behind me, so this made sense.

"Yeah, one day I walked home from school and saw all this new furniture and thought, 'Oh man, mom did some major redecorating while I was gone.'"

"Nooooooo," I say.

Kai goes on. "Then I went into another room, and I saw pictures of these white people, and I went, 'What the hell?' And then I remembered. This isn't our house anymore."

This isn't our house anymore.

Whew. This statement is loaded with sorrow and sullied by shame. I've said it to myself a million times. But never out loud, only in the dream I had over and over again.

In it, I walk through the kitchen door and set the groceries down, mouthwatering at the thought of deliciousness in those bags. I take a few extra steps until I gasp and say, "This isn't our house anymore."

I tell Kai about the uncanny resemblance of my dream to his reality.

"What happened next?" I ask, afraid he will tell me about an embarrassing run-in with the new owners.

"I just tiptoed out the way I came," he says with a smile.

"You did?" I ask incredulously. "You walked into the house that wasn't ours anymore, looked around, and left the way you came like nothing happened?"

I need to know I heard him right, seeing that I'm having difficulty separating his real-life story from my nightmare.

"Yup, I just walked out," Kai repeats, cracking himself up this time.

In my dream, I never left the scene. I stayed frozen in horror every time. And suddenly, I realize part of me is frozen in horror in my awake life, too. Part of me still thinks the divorce never should've happened, that my kids never should've had to leave the only home they'd known until then, pack up, and move next door.

Part of me thinks that I failed at being a mother.

All this is true, even though I've re-homed us to a place Kai and Reina love. Until this very moment,

unfreezing and walking out the door
hadn't even been a possibility that
crossed my mind. Is it? Can I?
I glance at Kai. Those punishing
thoughts are already melting away at
the edges. As ice turns to water, weight
comes off my shoulders, and my limbs
loosen up.

The answer is *yes*, and *I can*.

In my mind's eye, I follow Kai out of the
house—and climb into this car, where I
sit beside him, breathing in his
effervescent laughter.

Kai said, "Oops," and carried on.

PARTING WORDS + A RECIPE

I was gathering the last stories for this book when I came across this introductory note about miso soup.

"Miso soup is about comfort and being warmed from the inside out. My daughter, Reina, calls it 'a hug in a cup.'

Miso soup is meant to settle our nerves, so why get hung up on how to do it correctly? Why turn the making of comfort into an unsettling experience? The soup you make is infinitely better than the soup you don't."

*

One morning, I woke up craving a simple Japanese breakfast. Rice, check. Greens, check. Now, all I needed for a complete meal was soup. But then, my monkey mind started screaming—

You're behind schedule already!
Are you procrastinating writing?
Who has time for cooking...

Truth be told, I was procrastinating. Here I was, closing the book, still as foggy about what's worth wanting as ever. All I knew for sure was this:

When you acknowledge your story, warts and all, its beauty—and a clear sense of direction and priorities—rise to meet you.

I wanted to watch the steam rise to meet me. That was reason enough to want to make soup, so I did. And so it is for you, too: your wanting is reason enough for anything. Make steam rise.

"A Hug in a Cup" Easy Miso Soup

Serves 2

Dashi powder,* one packet
Miso paste,** one tablespoon
Water, 12 oz (30ml)
Scallion, 1-2, the green parts only thinly sliced

---

1. Bring the water to boil in a saucepan.

2. Remove from heat. Add the packet of dashi powder.

3. While the pan is off the heat, dissolve the miso into the dashi broth

(It's best to scoop some liquid into a ladle and dissolve the miso paste inside the ladle using cooking chopsticks.)

4. Return the pan to the burner on medium-high. Rewarm to the point of tiny bubbles forming at the edges (do not boil!)

5. Turn off the heat, add the scallions, and serve!

6. Alternately, put the dashi and miso in a cup, add boiling water, stir it up, and call it a job well done.

Note: You can add a pinch of freeze-dried wakame and cubed silken tofu at Step 4 for a classic miso soup.

Dashi powder*. The classic ingredients are a bonito and kelp (konbu) combo. Vegan options are plentiful, too. Look for dashi at any local brick-and-mortar Asian market or an online store.

ACKNOWLEDGMENTS

THANK YOU. My heart is bursting with gratitude for everyone I named below —and many more.

Bernadette Jiwa and Enrika Greathouse, without the Story Republic, the community you birthed, the courage to unearth and share these stories would've never come to me.

Alexandra Franzen and Lindsey Smith, Look what you started! There are now two books in my name because of you.

Joanna Bloor, you were ambitious for me from the beginning. I am such a lucky beneficiary of your fairy godmother magic.

Ross Gay, you don't know me, but someday you will, and I'll tell you how much your definition of essay—to try—has meant to me. May the book world flourish with an abundance of delightful "essay-ette" collections.

Alex Elle, you told me to stay rooted in love. I listened.

I am surrounded by astoundingly generous writers and storytellers from all over the world. Amanda, Michelle, Michael, April, Gary, Andrea, Kellie, Jacquie, Jackie, Sabah, Terry, Anne, Cat, Dave, Lyle, Sara, Sarah, Donald, Diane, Dingding, and Susan. You make my world turn.

Leanne Fournier, you inspired the subtitle; Caroline Harvey, you lovingly quoted me back; and Beth Pagano, you fed me a steady diet of ridiculously wonderful memes daily.

I am part of a mastermind group that's been running for eleven years strong! Jen, Terrace, Ursula. Namaste. You are my bedrock.

A shout-out to just a few of my fellow mothers who lived some of the stories with me: Cat, Lisa, Roberta, My Linh, Julie, Kimberly, and Marian. Yay, us.

Erika, you gave me a precious head start on mothering.

Pete, you help me remember what matters most.

Kai and Reina, you matter. You matter. You matter.

Scan me for book club & journaling prompts + other great resources. →

ABOUT THE AUTHOR

Rumi Tsuchihashi is the author of *I Want To Remember This: Recognizing The Tiny Moments That Make Up a Life,* and the essay 'Where Our Palms Touch,' featured in the Modern Love column of *The New York Times*.

As a copywriter, Rumi delights in finding in her clients' throughlines and creating unforgettable messages and business stories with them. She also offers coaching to first-time book authors — and anyone who wants to author a new story of their lives through her company, Tiny Wonders.

When not typing up the latest issue of *Nudge*, her Substack newsletter, you can find Rumi cooking up a delicious mess at home in Seattle, Washington.

www.ingramcontent.com/pod-product-compliance
Lightning Source LLC
LaVergne TN
LVHW041611070526
838199LV00052B/3100